THE STORY OF
OFFSHORE OIL

Messner Books by Harry Edward Neal

THE STORY OF OFFSHORE OIL

THE PEOPLE'S GIANT: The Story of TVA

COMMUNICATION: From Stone Age to Space Age

DIARY OF DEMOCRACY: The Story of Political
    Parties in America

THE MYSTERY OF TIME

THE PROTECTORS: The Story of the Food and
    Drug Administration

SIX AGAINST CRIME: Treasury Agencies in Action

THE STORY OF
OFFSHORE
OIL

by Harry Edward Neal

*Illustrated with
photographs*

Julian Messner
New York

Published by Julian Messner, a Simon & Schuster Division of Gulf & Western Corporation. Simon & Schuster Building, 1230 Avenue of the Americas, New York, N.Y. 10020

Printed in the United States of America

Design by Ruth Bornschlegel

Library of Congress Cataloging in Publication Data

Neal, Harry Edward
     The story of offshore oil.
     SUMMARY: Discusses the formation, location, and extraction of offshore oil. Presents the life of roustabouts who live and work on rigs and the concerns of environmental groups.
     1. Oil well drilling, Submarine—Juvenile literature.—2. Petroleum in submerged lands—Juvenile literature. [1. Oil well drilling. 2. Petroleum]
I. Title.
TN871.3.N4   622'.33'82   77-11175
ISBN 0-671-32888-3

Dedicated to
Teri, Nancy, and Tracy Ann,
with grandfatherly love

Acknowledgments

This book could not have been written without the help and advice of many people. Here are some of those to whom I am especially indebted:

Henry A. Hill, Regional Manager of Exploration, Continental Oil Company, Houston, Texas.

Dr. Leslie Mack, Exploration Affairs Department, American Petroleum Institute, Washington, D. C.

Robert Gaines, Assistant Editor, Continental Oil Company, Stamford, Connecticut.

Ms. Pauline C. Butler, Photo Librarian, Continental Oil Company, Stamford, Connecticut.

Basil Rose, Drilling Superintendent, Continental Oil Company, New Orleans, Louisiana.

H. D. Haley, Division Manager, Continental Oil Company, New Orleans, Louisiana.

Herman Herrington, Louis McRainey, Harvey Brossard, and other crew members aboard Drilling Rig Salén No. 1 in the Gulf of Mexico.

C. R. Cunningham, Senior Vice President, Salén Offshore Drilling Company, Houston, Texas.

L. "Pat" Leech, Rig Manager, Salén Offshore Drilling Company, New Orleans, Louisiana.

G. L. Steen, Managing Editor, Mobil World Magazine, New York, New York.

Carol L. Cox, Exxon Company, Houston, Texas.

Stan French, Seismograph Service Corporation, Tulsa, Oklahoma.

Ms. Linzee Weld, Environmental Policy Center, Washington, D.C.

Contents

Getting There

The alarm clock went off at midnight. The young man who shut it off climbed out of bed, took a shower, then dressed. After breakfast, he went out into the cold, snowy December night, got into his car and headed eastward, out of Texas.

At the same time, five hundred miles away, another man climbed into his station wagon and drove into the freezing night.

Far away, in a different direction, a third man sped down the dark highway in his Jeep.

All three men were heading for the same place—Grand Isle, Louisiana. And other men from other places would join them there.

They were all going to work aboard an offshore oil-drilling rig in the Gulf of Mexico.

This is the kind of offshore oil-drilling rig on which the men were going to work.

11

The men had driven hundreds of miles in order to be ready to go to work at noon. At Grand Isle, they parked their cars, had breakfast, and waited to be taken out to the rig. Sometimes they went on a ten-passenger helicopter. But on this day they boarded a large, fast workboat for the twenty-mile journey into the Gulf of Mexico.

The workboat was quieter than the helicopter, so the men could talk and move around if they wanted to. The boat passed many small swampy islands and bayous. This was the delta of the Mississippi River. The men saw flocks of wild ducks and snow-white pelicans. A few dolphins played in the waves ahead of the boat.

As the men got farther out into the Gulf, they began to see many *offshore rigs* with their *platforms*, and tall *derricks*, where drilling was going on. Those on which drilling had finished and derricks were removed are also called platforms. There are almost three thousand of both kinds in the Gulf of Mexico.

Within two hours, the workboat reached the rig where the men worked. As the boat came alongside, the *crane* operator on the rig lowered the *birdcage*, a small round platform enclosed by wire cables to keep people from falling off. Two or three men at a time climbed aboard the birdcage and were hauled into the air, then lowered to the rig platform, or deck.

Once all the men were taken aboard, another group of workers left in the same way to go ashore. The crew that had just arrived would work from noon until midnight. The crew

Typical workboat for carrying people and supplies to and from offshore rigs and platforms.

The crane operator hauls men and supplies and helps move drill pipe.

The birdcage lifts men from workboat to platform.

that was leaving had worked the midnight until noon shift. After working on the rig for seven days, each crew got seven days off. Most of the men worked twelve hours each day. When their seven-day shift ended, they returned to their homes and families.

What did the men do after they got aboard the rig? They helped to drill holes thousands of feet beneath the sea, to get the petroleum, or oil, that is so necessary to our daily living.

2.

Finding Oil

How did oil get under the sea floor?

For millions of years, rivers carried tree branches, leaves, grass, bugs, animals, and other things into the sea. These sank to the sea floor. Tons of seaweed, fish, and all kinds of tiny sea creatures died and sank to the bottom, too. All this material was slowly buried by the mud, sand and clay that rivers brought to the ocean.

Pressure and heat from the weight of the new mud and material finally turned the mud into rock. This same pressure and heat changed the remains and skeletons of animals and plants into oil and natural gas. Because they are made from fossils—the long-buried remains of plants and animals—oil and natural gas are called *fossil fuels*. Natural gas

1.

Many millions of years ago, some seashores looked like this. The plants and animals of that time would look strange to us. There were no birds or flowers, only trees and bushes. The weather was nearly always warm and wet. Then some shores began slowly to sink.

2.

A few million years later, the forest was gone. Its remains—dead trees, branches, logs, animals' skeletons—lay buried at the bottom of the sea, under growing layers of sand and sea shells. As time passed, the layers of sand and shells became heavier and heavier, finally forming rocks at the bottom of the sea.

3.

The weight of the rocks pressed the ancient forest remains into a thin layer. The heat and pressure began to change the remains into oil. Drop by drop, the oil seeped down through cracks in the rocks, until it reached places where it could not get out. Millions of gallons of oil gathered together in some spots. Water from the sea above could not get in because the rocks were too thick. Today, when a drill reaches one of these spots, it releases the pressure and the oil shoots upward through the drill pipes.

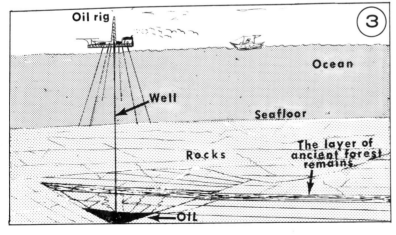

is similar to oil except that it is not a liquid—it is a gas. It is the gas used for cooking and heating.

As the population of the United States grew, the demand for gas and oil grew, too. Inventions and discoveries found other uses for gas and oil, and chemicals that came from oil, so that by the 1970s, Americans use something made from oil every day. Among them are toothpaste, soaps, wax paper, milk cartons, plastic dishes, many medicines, phonograph records, fishing tackle, asphalt tile, flavorings, waxes and polishes, synthetic fabrics and rubber, and thousands of other things.

More and more petroleum is needed to fill the ever-increasing demand, and oil companies must drill more wells to search for new supplies. One important source of oil is the rock layers under the ocean.

At first, wells could be drilled in water no deeper than two or three hundred feet. But new equipment has made it possible to work in much deeper places, farther out from the shore.

Oil under the sea is found mostly in Continental Shelf rocks. The *Continental Shelf* is all the land under the ocean from the shore out to about 600 feet deep. Every country that borders an ocean has a Continental Shelf, but it is always hidden by the sea.

The width of the Continental Shelf varies. Off the Atlantic Coast around New Jersey, it extends for nearly a hundred miles out. Off the Pacific Coast, however, the shelf

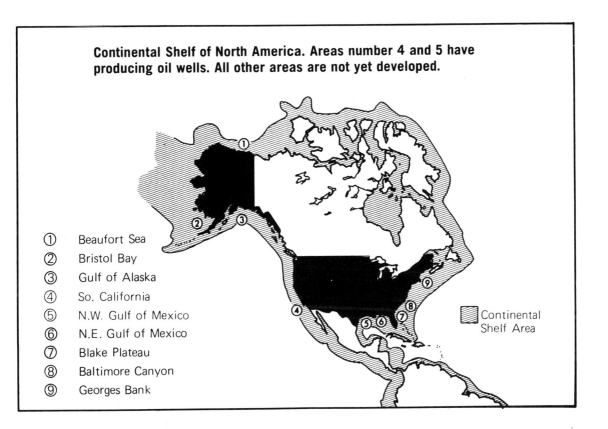

Continental Shelf of North America. Areas number 4 and 5 have producing oil wells. All other areas are not yet developed.

① Beaufort Sea
② Bristol Bay
③ Gulf of Alaska
④ So. California
⑤ N.W. Gulf of Mexico
⑥ N.E. Gulf of Mexico
⑦ Blake Plateau
⑧ Baltimore Canyon
⑨ Georges Bank

Continental Shelf Area

averages only eighteen miles wide. Along the Gulf of Mexico, it ranges from 4 to 130 miles.

The United States Continental Shelf is controlled by the federal government. An oil company that wants to do off-shore drilling must first get a government lease. This is a contract in which the government grants permission to the oil company to drill. In return, the oil company pays an agreed amount of money to the government.

Up until 1976, American offshore drilling was done only in the Gulf of Mexico, the Pacific Ocean, and Alaskan waters. But in 1976, the government granted leases to oil companies to drill in the Atlantic Ocean, off the New Jersey coast.

These oil companies, such as Exxon, Shell, Texaco and Conoco (Continental Oil Company), rent their drilling rigs from contractors who build and own them. Contractors name their rigs, and the one to which the men were taken on the workboat is called Salén No. 1. It is owned by the Salén Offshore Drilling Company, and cost 27 million dollars. Conoco rents Salén No. 1, and it costs them about $30,000 a day to operate the rig.

How does a company know where to drill for offshore oil? *Seismologists*, scientists who study earthquakes, use a special device, a capsule that is towed under water, and which gives out loud electronic claps like small explosions. The sound waves made by the claps go to the sea floor, bounce off rocks, and are returned upward as an echo to an instrument on the towing boat called a *seismograph*. The results are gone over by *geophysicists* and *geologists*, scientists who study the structure of the earth. From the kinds of rocks and the way they are formed, these scientists can guess where oil might be found by drilling.

But they can never be absolutely sure. The only sure

The exploration vessel *Seisjet* tows underwater device.

way is to drill a well. And even then, they do not know whether they will find oil, or natural gas, or both. So the oil company must decide whether to spend the great amounts of money needed to set up and operate a rig to search for oil. According to the oil industry, only one out of every fifty wells brings up enough oil to pay its drilling costs.

When drilling fails to produce oil, the well is called a *dry hole*. It is filled with cement, the platform is lowered to the water, and the rig is towed to some other location to continue the search.

3.

Rigs and Roustabouts

Salén No. 1 is a jack-up rig.

A *jack-up rig* is a huge floating rig and platform with very tall legs that can be lowered to the sea bottom in order to raise, or jack up the platform above the water.

Salén No. 1 was towed by a barge to its location off the coast of Louisiana. The platform floated like a raft, and the legs, about 300 feet long, stuck straight up in the air. Then the legs were lowered by electric motors 60 feet down to the sea floor, making the rig steady. The platform was raised, or jacked up like an automobile being repaired, until it was above the surface of the sea. Then it was no longer a floating rig. It sat on its legs on the bottom, with the platform above the water.

A jack-up drilling rig. On the Salén No. 1, the legs are so big around that a person could easily stand inside one.

DRILLING SHIP JACK-UP RIG

SEMI-SUBMERSIBLE RIG

Types of drilling rigs. Legs and base of semi-submersible rig are flooded and submerged to help provide stability.

There are two other kinds of rigs. One, called a *submersible*, operates in shallow water. The other, a *semi-submersible*, is used in very deep water. The semi-submersible is a true floating rig. Its legs do not reach the bottom.

For drilling wells in deep water, a *drill ship* is sometimes used instead of a rig. This is a self-propelled ship with

a drilling derrick, or mast, in the center. The ship carries all of the supplies and gear needed to drill a well.

Part of the deck of Salén No. 1 is used for helicopter landings and takeoffs. But all the rest of the space is given over to drilling equipment. There are stacks of long pieces of steel pipe, a drilling derrick, drilling engines, a crane, electric cables, tanks, and other gear. Wherever one looks, there is machinery.

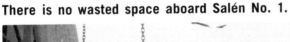

Semi-submersible rig used for drilling in waters 500 feet deep. Figure of the man (center) gives idea of the rig size.

There is no wasted space aboard Salén No. 1.

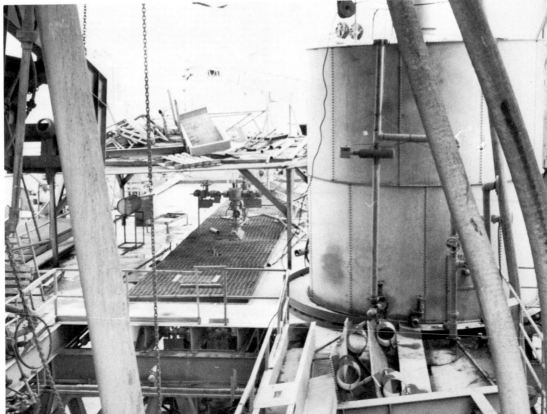

The December wind was brisk, and the *roustabouts* wore thermal jackets, heavy shoes and hard hats. Everyone must wear a hard hat outdoors on the rig.

Roustabouts are laborers—men and women. On Salén

Molly Jean Ritter, roustabout.

Roustabouts handle sections of heavy drill pipe. They work hard, getting about six dollars an hour, with more for overtime.

No. 1, they were all men. They piled and unpiled heavy bags of dried drilling mud. They worked with the crane operator to unload workboats that brought mud, pipes, cables and other supplies. They spliced and repaired cables. They handled sections of drill pipe that weighed as much as 600 pounds. They scraped old paint off parts of the rig and repainted those places. And they did many other kinds of cleanup jobs.

Work aboard the Salén No. 1 was supervised by a *tool pusher* or drilling superintendent. He worked closely with the drilling foreman, and both were on call 24 hours a day, in case of emergency.

4.

Getting the Oil

Salén No. 1 already had six wells producing oil, but at the same time, three new wells were being drilled in order to find more oil.

Some wells are drilled straight down, while others are drilled at an angle. To better understand, hold your hand downward and separate your fingers. Each finger represents a drill for a well, all from a single location.

The drilling on Salén No. 1 is done by a round steel *bit*, made up of three big, heavy wheels with teeth in them. The wheels of the bit are connected to an engine which makes them turn. The bit is fastened to the *string*, a long stretch of steel pipe sections that have been screwed together. The

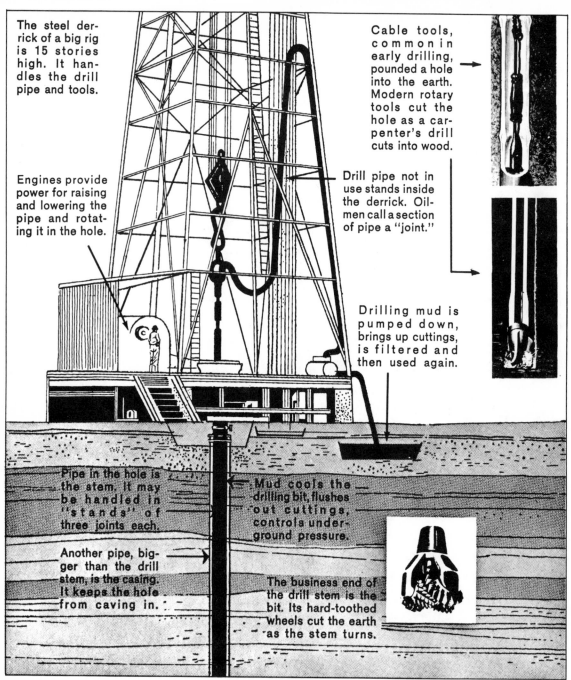

The steel derrick of a big rig is 15 stories high. It handles the drill pipe and tools.

Engines provide power for raising and lowering the pipe and rotating it in the hole.

Cable tools, common in early drilling, pounded a hole into the earth. Modern rotary tools cut the hole as a carpenter's drill cuts into wood.

Drill pipe not in use stands inside the derrick. Oilmen call a section of pipe a "joint."

Drilling mud is pumped down, brings up cuttings, is filtered and then used again.

Pipe in the hole is the stem. It may be handled in "stands" of three joints each.

Mud cools the drilling bit, flushes out cuttings, controls underground pressure.

Another pipe, bigger than the drill stem, is the casing. It keeps the hole from caving in.

The business end of the drill stem is the bit. Its hard-toothed wheels cut the earth as the stem turns.

Drilling continues night and day as the well slowly sinks.

The bit will bite its way into the earth and rock of the sea floor.

string hangs inside a casing called the *conductor pipe*. A crane inside the drilling derrick lowers the string to the well, and a drilling engine turns the string and the wheels of the bit, which bites its way into the earth and rock of the sea floor.

When the bit goes as deep as the string allows, more pipe is added. The *roughnecks* who lengthen the pipe must be big and strong, because it is hard work.

Opposite and below: Roughnecks separate the drill pipe and prepare to add a new length.

About once every 25 or 30 hours, the drilling derrick crane pulls the string up so that the drill bit can be changed. Bits get worn down after a while, and do not cut too well. It may take roughnecks as long as 24 hours to complete the change, called a *trip*.

Roughnecks also take care of the drilling engines and mud pumps.

To keep the bit cool and the string running freely, mud is pumped into the conductor pipe. It isn't just ordinary mud-puddle mud. It looks like thick hot chocolate and works like lubricating oil. It's a form of clay that is mixed with water and several chemicals.

The mud is heavy enough so that when pieces of rock or other material are cut by the bit, they are lifted to the top of the conductor pipe and into a waste pit. If water or oil were used for lubrication, the chunks of rock or other trash might clog the hole. Geologists can tell from the kinds of rock that come up whether oil has been found or whether deeper drilling is needed.

Below the platform is a mud logging room. There a mud engineer and a *mud logger* make sure that the mud mixture is the right weight and thickness before it is pumped into the conductor pipe. If the mud is too heavy, it might stop up the pipe. If it isn't heavy enough, there could be a blowout and the oil would spill into the water.

Everything on the rig is aimed at safety, not only for the workers, but also for the wells. Working around rig machinery is always a risk, and everyone tries to watch out for

This tank supplies and controls drilling mud.

Escape capsule holds 28 people. It is motor driven and, in an emergency, can get them away from the rig quickly.

everyone else. A typical accident usually involves cut or mashed fingers. Most accidents happen around the revolving table that turns the drill pipe. And the possibility of a blowout is always a cause for worry.

A *blowout* means that oil from a well being drilled is out of control. The pressure is so great that the oil erupts, creating a "wild well," or *gusher*. The result might be an oil spill that could seriously pollute water and beaches, as happened near Santa Barbara, California, in 1969. The spilled oil can kill fish and sea birds, and make water and beaches unfit for swimming.

Blowouts are rare now, because drillers do everything possible to prevent them. One of the most important mechanical means is a blowout preventer. This is a device that can shut down the well completely.

Blowout preventers are devices to control any unexpected pressures that may occur during the drilling of an oil well. Here, a blowout preventer is inspected before it is installed on an offshore well in the Gulf of Mexico.

Another kind of blowout preventer blocks the space between the drill string and the conductor pipe, under water, to keep the pressure down. Then heavier drilling mud is pumped into the conductor to control the pressure.

Also, there are emergency switches on the platform that could stop all machinery, if necessary.

On Salén No. 1, the bit was already 7,600 feet down. It will go to 9,370 feet, because that's where geologists believe oil will be found. Some wells in other parts of the ocean are 25,000 feet deep—almost five miles!

When oil is found, the drilling stops. The bit and string are pulled out of the hole, and a pipe called a *production casing* is put into the hole and cemented in place. Another pipe, called *tubing*, is put inside the casing. The oil will be pumped through the tubing, which is connected to valves on a *Christmas tree*. The Christmas tree is on the platform. It is a large upright pipe with valves sticking out all over it, like tree branches. These control the flow of oil from the producing well.

Oil is collected in tanks aboard the rig. Then it is pumped through a pipeline on the ocean floor, either to tanks on shore or to a *gathering station*. A gathering station is a platform in the sea with large tanks. Oil from several producing wells may be pumped first to the gathering station and then to tanks ashore, ready to go to refineries.

When wells produce natural gas instead of oil, the gas is sent through different pipelines to tanks on shore.

This onshore "Christmas tree" is similar to one on an offshore oil platform.

There are many regulations that govern the drilling of offshore oil wells in the United States. All the oil companies must obey the rules and regulations of government agencies, including the U.S. Geological Survey, the Coast Guard,

Opposite: A barge in the Gulf of Mexico lays connecting pipeline to bring oil ashore from the drilling rig.

Below: Grand Isle pumping station.

the Fish and Wildlife Service, the Environmental Protection Agency, the Army's Corps of Engineers, and the Bureau of Land Management, among others. All of these agencies are concerned about safety and the environment. These areas are growing in importance because new parts of the oceans are being opened up for offshore drilling.

5.

Life Aboard the Rig

On board Salén No. 1, the cooks help to keep the workers happy by serving plenty of good food. All food is provided and prepared by a catering company whose cooks and kitchen helpers live aboard the rig.

Tenderloin and sirloin steaks are favorites, along with pork chops, roast beef, chicken, shrimp, fish and seafood gumbo, a kind of stew that is a Louisiana specialty. Ice cream, fresh-baked pies, cakes, bread and rolls, tea, coffee, milk and soft drinks are on hand at all times. There is no beer, wine or liquor, because alcoholic beverages aren't permitted.

The rig has a drinking fountain, a coffee urn and an ice cream machine. The water in the drinking fountain is fresh

The galley of an offshore rig where meals are prepared.

Good meals are a highlight of each working day.

water made from sea water that has had the salt removed by "watermakers" on board the rig.

Four meals a day are served on Salén No. 1. The fourth meal is really breakfast for the shift that goes to work at midnight, as well as those who are coming off duty who may also be hungry.

Caterers also supply towels and linens and make up the men's bunks, just as though the workers were guests in a

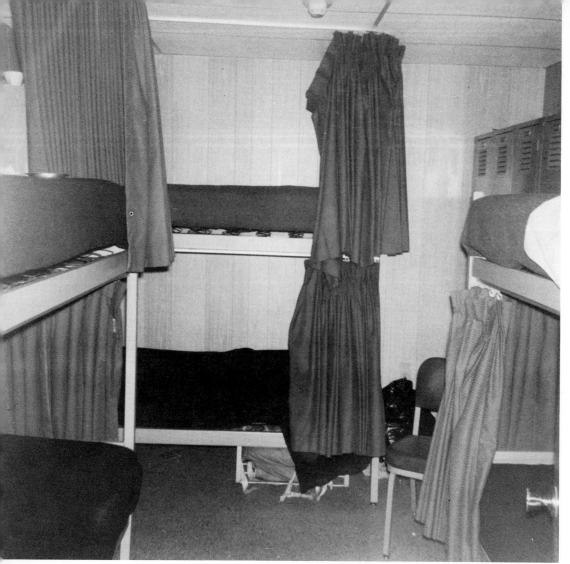

A six-bunk bedroom aboard Salén No. 1.

hotel. The beds are two-tiered bunks, six bunks to a room. Each bunk has a curtain for privacy. Nearby is a shower room.

There is a sewage treatment plant aboard the rig, so

that toilets and other wastes do not pollute the ocean. Garbage is sorted, trash collected, put into metal containers, and later taken ashore to be gotten rid of.

No matter where the men go on the rig, they can hear the muffled sound of pump motors and other machinery. But they quickly become used to the sound and vibrations.

After a day's work, the drilling crew usually read or play cards, checkers, or dominoes. Gambling is not permitted. Others smoke and sip soft drinks while they watch television. Smoking is not allowed outdoors on the platform. Some workers write letters, or just sit around and talk.

Once in a while, a rare species of bird lands on the rig to rest. When that happens, the "camera bugs" among the crew members get pictures of the visitor.

Some of the men enjoy fishing from the rig, and the fishing is excellent. Why? In many parts of the oceans, there are natural reefs that attract fish. But there are few such natural reefs in the Gulf of Mexico off the Louisiana coast. Instead, the oil platforms have become reefs—artificial ones. Barnacles and other small sea creatures attach themselves to the steel legs and are eaten by small fish. The small fish, in turn, attract big fish, and the big fish attract fishermen who fish for sport and also for a living.

Often there are fishing boats close by the rigs. The fishermen catch red snapper, weakfish, white trout, croaker, tarpon, Spanish and king mackerel, grouper, bluefish, shark, barracuda, pompano, and other varieties. Some may weigh 400 pounds or more. If a member of the drilling crew

On their off-duty time, crew members often fish from the rig.

should hook a 400-pounder, it can always be hauled aboard by the crane operator. Some crew members keep fish in the freezer and take them home on their next time off.

Although the men don't communicate regularly with their families on land, they keep in touch by radio aboard the rig. Marine operators all along the coast connect the radio with land telephone lines.

Weather is very important to workers on an offshore drilling platform, and they pay close attention to forecasts. Sometimes hurricanes roar into the Gulf of Mexico, and the rigs are battered by huge waves and pelted by heavy rains. Gale force winds can easily blow a man off the rig. When damaging storms occur, drilling and other activity stops for a while. Sometimes when hurricanes are forecast, most of the rig workers are taken ashore and lodged in motels until the danger is past.

Offshore workers are concerned about the weather, for gale force winds can be dangerous.

6.

Environmentalists vs Oil Companies

The oil the United States gets from its own offshore and onshore (land) wells just isn't enough to supply the country's needs. So finding new sources of oil is very important. Much of our oil is imported from Nigeria, Venezuela, and especially from Middle East countries such as Saudi Arabia, Iran and Kuwait. If the United States can find enough oil on its own Continental Shelf, it will not have to depend so heavily upon these nations.

However, many onshore wells that have been producing oil for years are drying up. And land where new wells might be drilled is getting hard to find. A new and very large oil field was discovered in Alaska in 1968, and oil started flowing in 1977. But it will not be enough so long as our demand for oil keeps going up. We will still have to rely on imported oil.

Experts believe that billions of barrels of oil can be found by more offshore drilling. That's why the federal government has, for the first time, let oil companies explore for oil along the Atlantic Coast, just as they have been doing on the Pacific and Gulf coasts.

The Environmental Policy Center, of Washington, D.C., and many other such groups, realize that we must have oil. And since drilling must go on, there is always the danger of spills. When there are spills from pipelines or wells offshore, the oil companies responsible must pay for cleaning up.

Experimental Lockheed oil skimmer can sweep up as much as 1,000 gallons of spilled oil per minute.

Burning oil can also pollute the ocean. The U.S. Coast Guard
Cutter *Dependable* assists at a burning rig off the Louisiana coast in the Gulf of Mexico. The fire which began December 1, 1970 was not extinguished until April 12, 1971.

On February 8, 1969, a blowout occurred in an offshore oil well in Santa Barbara Channel, California, causing an 800-mile oil slick and ruining some 40 miles of beaches and killing a large number of birds and fish. This was the most serious oil spill to take place off American shores.

The danger of oil spills has led other environmental groups to fight against any offshore drilling. A blowout in an offshore well in the North Sea in April, 1977, leaked oil into the ocean at the rate of 47,000 gallons per hour. Up to that time, however, there had been only four major oil spills due to offshore drilling. At least one of these resulted from a break in the pipeline that carried oil from a rig to the shore. When such a pipeline springs a leak, divers are brought in to locate it and repair the pipe. But until they do, oil keeps leaking into the ocean.

The oil companies say that oil spills do not cause permanent damage to beaches, or to fish and wildlife. Even with a major spill, the companies say that cleanup operations will finally clear away the mess.

The National Research Council claims, however, that heavy damage has happened in some areas. They go on to say that we really do not know yet if oil pollution has reached a dangerous level. It will take years to study the effects on the environment and wildlife.

Scientists of the Woods Hole Oceanographic Institution in Massachusetts made studies of an oil spill off the Massachusetts coast. Their laboratory experiments showed that the damage caused by the oil lasts a long time. The scientists said that the dangers to fish and other food sources created by oil spills were far greater than they had expected. They also reported that oil can still be found in sea creatures after all signs of spilled oil have gone. And poisonous chemicals from oil may stay in the sea for months after a spill.

Environmentalists say that offshore drilling may change beaches and coastal areas into eyesores with their storage tanks and pumping stations. The oil companies reply that most of the land needed for refineries and other buildings could be located far away from beaches and recreation areas.

The people who live in Atlantic coastal towns are afraid

that bringing oil ashore from offshore wells will pollute the beaches and inlets, and kill sea birds and fish. The oil industry says that the offshore oil would be brought to land by pipelines that are buried wherever they cross beach areas.

Miles of ugly tide lines are engraved on the beach at Yorktown, Virginia, by oil swept ashore from a tanker's bilges emptied into the York River. An oil smothered turtle disturbs a boy who once enjoyed the water sports and wild life here.

There is danger of oil pollution from other sources, too. Barges carrying thousands of gallons of oil have had accidents that have dumped the oil into the sea or rivers. Tankers loaded with millions of gallons of oil have run aground or have been broken up in storms, leaving their cargoes to flow into the water over a distance of many miles. Tanker operators also dump oil into the oceans when they clean their tanks. This practice has been declared illegal by many countries, but it still goes on.

With more drilling off the Atlantic Coast, environmentalists are fearful of what may happen to towns in the coastal areas. They believe that if large groups of oil workers and their families arrive, there will be a great demand for houses, roads, schools, utilities, more firemen and policemen, more shopping centers and recreation. Many towns can't provide these things quickly. And some towns don't want such fast growth.

The oil companies answer that the economy of the towns would improve. There would be more jobs for people who already live in the area. Local merchants and other business people would also profit. And new homeowners as well as businesses would contribute more tax money to the communities.

So what do we do now?

We can develop solar and nuclear energy, but it will be years before these are in wide use. We can use coal, but burning coal causes pollution. The fact is that at some future day, our oil and natural gas wells may dry up. But we need oil and gas now, so we must conserve what we have until new sources can be found.

Despite all the warnings of shortages and waste, there are people who still do not believe that we are running out of energy. President Carter has stated: "With the exception of preventing war, this is the greatest challenge that our country will face during our lifetimes. The energy crisis has not yet overwhelmed us, but it will if we do not act quickly."

In other words, we must stop wasting energy, or the time will come when we can no longer provide light, heat and power for our homes, our schools, our transportation, and our industries.

Glossary

BIRDCAGE—a small round platform for hauling workers on and off the rig. It is enclosed with wire so no one can fall out, and it is raised or lowered by the crane on the rig.

BLOWOUT—an explosive gushing out of oil and natural gas. It happens when a drill suddenly bites through a rock layer into an oil deposit that lies under the rock, and under heavy pressure from the weight of the rock. The oil is released and shoots up through the hole to the surface, sometimes blowing away part of the derrick.

CASING—a pipe that is put into the drill hole after oil has been found.

CHRISTMAS TREE—a large upright pipe with valves and branch pipes sticking out like the branches of a tree.

COAL—a rock fuel, found in underground layers in many parts of the world. It is a fossil fuel, formed over millions of years from the remains of living things.

CONDUCTOR PIPE—also called a casing, the outer pipe in a drill hole. It forms the wall of the drill hole. The drill pipe fits inside the conductor pipe.

CONTINENTAL SHELF—all the land along the coast of a continent which lies under the ocean, to a depth of about 600 feet.

CRANE—a machine with a long swinging arm, for lifting and moving heavy loads. It is used on a rig for lifting heavy supplies and the birdcage. *See also* derrick.

DERRICK—the towering steel frame on the rig, directly over the well hole. It is really a kind of crane, used for lowering and raising the string and bit.

DRILL SHIP—a ship with a big hole in its bottom. Drill pipes and bit can be lowered to the sea floor through the hole. A drill ship is used to drill wells in very deep water.

DRY HOLE—a well that does not bring up oil.

ENERGY—the power to do work.

ENVIRONMENT—everything around you: air, water, sunshine, streets, animals, plants, houses, and so on.

ENVIRONMENTALIST—a person who is interested in protecting nature.

FOSSIL FUEL—any fuel made from fossils, the long-buried remains of plants and animals. Oil, natural gas and coal are fossil fuels.

GASOLINE—one of several light, flammable fuels that is a part of oil. It is separated from the oil by chemical means, and used mainly to drive the engines of most cars, trucks, buses and airplanes.

GATHERING STATION—a place where pipes from many different oil wells come together. The oil from all the pipes is gathered into several larger pipelines for movement to storage tanks which may be miles away.

GEOLOGIST—a scientist who studies the earth.

GEOPHYSICIST—a scientist who studies the way matter behaves.

GUSHER—an oil well that gives oil in great amounts. Natural gas may also be present.

JACK-UP RIG—a floating rig and its platform with tall legs which are lowered to the sea bottom when the rig reaches the drilling site. Then the platform is raised, or jacked up, to above the surface of the water.

MUD LOGGER—the person whose job it is to mix and control the quality of the mud which is being pumped down into the well to help cool the bit and keep the pipe free of rocks and trash that might clog it up.

NATURAL GAS—a fossil fuel often found with oil. It is similar to oil, except that it is not a liquid, but is an invisible gas, just like the gas used in most homes for heating and cooking.

NUCLEAR ENERGY—the energy contained in the nucleus of an atom.

OFFSHORE—the shallow coastal water of the Continental Shelf.

ONSHORE—the mainland.

PETROLEUM—a fossil fuel that is pumped from wells deep in the earth. It is an oily, dark-colored liquid and contains many different chemicals and gases.

PLATFORM—the level working surface of a drill rig. Sometimes the word is used to mean the whole rig.

POLLUTION—anything which dirties the environment.

RIG—everything at the offshore drilling site, including the platform, legs and all the equipment and machines.

ROUGHNECKS—men who lift the heavy pipes and fit them into the well to lengthen the string.

ROUSTABOUTS—any of the workers on the rig, such as repairmen, painters, carriers, pipe handlers, and others.

SEISMOGRAPH—a scientific instrument that records vibrations from small electronic explosions which geologists set off under water. The kind of vibrations that are recorded help geologists tell where oil can be found.

SEMI-SUBMERSIBLE—a floating rig used in deep water for drilling a well.

SOLAR ENERGY—the rays of light and heat from the sun, which can be controlled in such a way as to heat water, produce electricity, or even melt steel.

STRING—all the sections of pipe that have been "strung" together inside the conductor pipe.

TANKER—a specially built ship for carrying petroleum by sea.

TOOL PUSHER—an oil driller's name for a drilling superintendent, a supervising officer.

TRIP—a name for the whole series of actions that complete a change of the drill bit. One trip may take as long as 24 hours to complete.

WORKBOAT—a boat for ferrying workers between the mainland and the offshore rigs.

Index